ALLEN COUNTY PUBLIC LIBRARY

3 1833 09760 6293

YO-CYP-458

The Picture Story of
Jockey STEVE CAUTHEN

The Picture Stor

# of Jockey

STEVE CAUTHEN

by Anne Marie Mueser

Illustrated with photographs

JULIAN MESSNER NEW YORK

Copyright © 1979 by Anne Mueser Associates, Ltd.

All rights reserved including the right of reproduction in whole or in part in any form. Published by Julian Messner, a Simon & Schuster Division of Gulf & Western Corporation, Simon & Schuster Building, 1230 Avenue of the Americas, New York, N.Y. 10020.

Manufactured in the United States of America

Design by Alex D'Amato

Library of Congress Cataloging in Publication Data

Mueser, Anne Marie.
    The picture story of jockey Steve Cauthen.

    SUMMARY: A biography emphasizing the career of the 18-year-old jockey who led Affirmed to a Triple Crown victory in 1978.
    1. Cauthen, Steve, 1960-   —Juvenile literature.
2. Jockeys—United States—Biography—Juvenile literature. [1. Cauthen, Steven, 1960-   2. Jockeys]
I. Title.
SF336.C38M83   798'.43'0924 [B] [92]   78-27884
ISBN 0-671-32990-1

This book is dedicated to children everywhere who love horses— and especially to Cameron, the best Connemara pony in South Devon, and to Tommy, who runs whether or not there's a race.

CO. SCHOOLS
C869068

ACKNOWLEDGMENTS

Many people helped in the preparation of THE PICTURE STORY OF STEVE CAUTHEN, I would especially like to thank the following:

Don Smith and Hy Hollinger, for introducing me to Steve Cauthen . . .

Liz Naples, for being in the right place at the right time with her camera . . .

Joyce's Steak House, for serving as an office and a second home . . .

Nat Andriani of UPI, for providing photographs . . .

Lee Hoffman, for getting the project started . . .

Madelyn Anderson, for superb editing . . .

The Goodmans, for helping to make Steve's life such a great story, and for their kindness . . .

Len and Ellen Cole, and Susan Baker, for their encouragement and continued support . . .

and most of all,

Steve Cauthen, for his love of horses, his skill, and his style—all of which add up to a life story unlikely to be equaled.

AMM

Jockey Steve Cauthen drives Affirmed home to win the Kentucky Derby.

*E*ach year, on the first Saturday in May, a great crowd gathers at Churchill Downs in Louisville, Kentucky, to watch a race that has been called the most exciting two minutes in sports—the Kentucky Derby. The season's best three-year-old race horses compete in the Run for the Roses, the first event in racing's highly prized Triple Crown: the Derby, the Preakness, the Belmont Stakes.

On May 6, 1978, more than 130,000 people were at Churchill Downs for the 104th running of the Kentucky Derby. There was a special excitement in the air—even more than usual for Derby Day. Two great horses were competing—Alydar, a local Kentucky steed, and Affirmed, a horse raised in California. Alydar was a slight favorite, but many people thought Affirmed to be the better horse. The crowd expected a tight race.

The contest wasn't even close. Affirmed, with Jockey Steve Cauthen in the saddle, won the race by a length and a half, as the crowd roared. Winning the Kentucky Derby is every jockey's dream, although most jockeys don't even get a chance to ride in the famous race. Steve Cauthen not only rode but won his very first Run for the Roses. It was a victory that came five days past his 18th birthday.

Steve Cauthen grew up in a family that loves horses. The Cauthen family's influence on Steve's career can be traced directly to his parents, Myra and Ronald Cauthen. At the age of 13, Ronald "Tex" Cauthen began working with horses. It was a job he preferred to working on the family farm. He had to break and train half-wild quarter horses, and Tex bit the dust often as he learned his new trade. At sixteen, Tex went on to work with racehorses, and he has been a "racetracker" ever since.

Steve's mother, Myra Cauthen, is a "race-tracker" as well as a homemaker. She trains horses at small tracks in Ohio, close to the Cauthen home in Kentucky. Horses are a way of life for the Cauthens. It was Steve's mother who first put him up on a horse, when the boy was only two.

Three-year-old Steve Cauthen sits aboard a horse at the family farm in Walton, Kentucky. He was a fearless rider even as a toddler.

When asked once if he had always wanted to be a jockey, Steve quickly replied, "Oh no, you don't dare hope for that until you know you're not going to be too big." He said that he had always known he would do something with horses, but that he was twelve years old before he was sure he would be small enough to be a jockey.

Long before he decided he wanted to be a race rider, Steve had learned the many basics about the care and handling of racehorses. He learned to clean and groom a horse to perfection. He learned how to get a horse ready for a race and how to care for the animal after the race was over. And, he learned to ride.

Steve Cauthen is a natural on a horse. Since he rode his first pony, he has always appeared to be at home on the back of a horse. His quiet manner with the animals shows in the way they behave for him. A nervous rider often upsets a horse. Steve, on the other hand, has a calming effect on the animals he rides.

When Steve was only seven, a trainer at

Latonia, Kentucky, race track jokingly asked the lad if he'd like to ride Slade, a stallion almost impossible to handle around the stable. The trainer hadn't really intended to let the child get on Slade, but Steve begged for the chance. The boy not only rode the headstrong animal around the barn, but came back laughing.

Not all of Steve's education as a race rider occurred on the back of a live horse. It was in the barn behind the Cauthen house in Walton, Kentucky that Steve practiced and perfected the skills of holding the reins and the whip.

A set of leather reins is still attached to a nail in the loft of the barn where Steve learned the feel of the reins and how to handle them. His horses in these practice sessions were bales of hay. Steve spent many hundreds of hours sitting on bales, slashing away at the hay, switching the whip from one hand to the other, and learning to hit the exact spot he wanted every time.

Steve explained the importance of using a whip effectively in successful race riding. "I'd

Steve shows his skill with the whip at the finish line.

like children who read this book to understand," he said, "that using a whip on a race horse isn't cruel. You need to get the horse's attention. It doesn't hurt."

The way Steve handles the reins and the whip in a race shows the benefit of the early years of practice and more practice. Many an expert observer has commented on Steve's amazing hands and how well the young jockey communicates messages to the horse through the reins. And the many bales of hay that Steve broke apart while practicing his whip handling skills have paid off in what now appears to be an almost effortless handling of the whip in a race.

When Steve Cauthen was twelve, he told his father that he wanted to be a race rider. No one in the family was surprised. Tex Cauthen, who knew that his son's desire was a real one and not an idle dream, encouraged the boy to develop his talents fully. Tex took Steve to the River Downs track and showed the boy the starting gate. Steve spent many afternoons watching and studying how to get a horse speedily out of the gate without any mistakes.

At River Downs, Steve observed and timed many workouts and races. He learned the importance of judging the exact pace needed to win a race without taking too much out of the horse. These many hours of watching and timing gave Steve what many people refer to as a "clock in the head," an instinctive ability to judge pace and to use that judgment successfully while riding a race horse.

Steve and his father watched dozens of films of races run at Latonia and River Downs. They studied the films over and over again. They talked about the good and bad parts of each race, and how to avoid the mistakes that other riders had made.

Steve worked hard on developing his own special style of riding. While many jockeys appear to be constantly in motion as they urge a horse on, Cauthen sits quietly and calmly. He rides low on the horse with his back still and

Steve's position on a horse is low and steady.

straight. It has been said that a cup of tea on Steve's back during a race probably wouldn't spill. Steve's style makes sense. He sits low so that he keeps wind resistance down as much as possible. This gives the horse an extra advantage. Steve's riding style wastes no energy. Every move he makes has a purpose.

During this entire time that Steve Cauthen was learning the race business, he was also attending school with the other boys and girls his age. Steve was an average student, who preferred to spend his time learning about horses rather than doing his homework. His parents insisted, however, that Steve apply himself and do well in school. When they told him he had to do well or they wouldn't permit him to get a jockey's license, Steve worked harder at his studies and raised his average to better than a B.

Steve Cauthen celebrated his sixteenth birthday on Derby Day, May 1, 1976. At last Steve was old enough to be eligible for a license to ride. Perhaps even more important, he had learned more about race riding by the age of sixteen than some jockeys could learn in a lifetime at the track. Steve Cauthen was ready to be a race rider, and that was what he wanted most.

On May 12, 1976, Steve Cauthen rode in his first official race at Churchill Downs. How did Steve feel? When he walked into the paddock to get ready, he looked fine. Any outsider, if asked, would probably have commented on how calm the kid seemed to be. Perhaps it was only Steve's mother who knew that under the quiet, calm expression there was a bit of nervousness.

Myra Cauthen gives her son a hug as he gets ready for a race.

It was a big day. And while Steve may have been a little bit anxious, his mother was downright scared. Myra Cauthen looked at her son and wondered why she had let him do it. She still recalls the fear she felt in her stomach before her son's first race.

Cauthen's mount in this race, a horse named King of Swat, was a long shot and was not expected to do much at all. Steve rode well, however, and the horse, not fit for distance, performed just as expected. Steve summed up the race by saying, "He ran well. And then he stopped." That's just what happened. The horse ran well at the start, but he tired early and finished next to last.

Steve's second race of the day, on another horse with little or no chance to win, was a fine one, although he again finished out of the money. But he had gotten through his first day as a real jockey, and his career was off and running.

Breaking in as a jockey is tough. Many trainers don't want to risk letting a new, inexperienced rider on their horses. To make it a little easier for beginners, the racing rules permit an apprentice to ride with less weight than a regular jockey. Some horses perform better with as little weight on them as possible, and their trainers would be attracted to a good apprentice. A rider can race with ten pounds less weight added to his or her gear until the fifth win. An apprentice continues to get a weight allowance for a year after the fifth win. Until the 35th victory, the allowance is seven pounds. After that, it's five pounds. Some jockeys take months to win five races. Some never do. It took Steve Cauthen exactly two weeks.

Five days after Steve's first race at Churchill Downs, Tex Cauthen decided to move his son to River Downs, the smaller track closer to home. It was easier for the boy to get mounts at the small track where he and his parents were well known, and where there was less competition. After the move to River Downs, Steve's first winning race wasn't long in coming.

On May 17, 1976, in the featured eighth race at River Downs, Steve was aboard a horse named

Weighing in.

Red Pipe. The distance for the race was a short one, and the track was muddy and slow. Steve's instructions from the trainer were to let the horse relax and run easily, and then to make one strong move with three furlongs (three-eighths of a mile) to go. Steve rode Red Pipe firmly and confidently, and followed the plan exactly. At the three-eighths pole, and fifteen lengths behind, Steve made his move. It worked. Red Pipe came in a length and a half ahead of the field, and the young jockey had his first win.

This first victory for Steve Cauthen was a special occasion for the entire family, his parents, his younger brothers, Doug and Kerry, and his uncle, Tommy Bischoff, the trainer of Red Pipe. Steve remembers vividly the day and the details. As is the custom when any new jockey wins his first race, the other riders in the jockey room yelled and cheered and covered Steve with shaving cream, shoe polish, and anything else they could find to mess him up. It was all laughs and shouts of joy as Steve went to the showers on this exciting day of his first race victory.

Steve kept right on winning races at River Downs. By the time school let out for the summer vacation, Steve had gone from being an unknown high school junior to being the sensation of the River Downs track. In the track's 56-day summer meeting, Steve rode a record 96 winners. His total of 120 winners for the season also broke the previous River Downs record of 103 victories.

The Winner's Circle was to become a habit for Steve Cauthen.

At this point, Steve Cauthen seemed to be ready to move on to a better track and more competition than River Downs could offer. The boy had already proved that he was an excellent rider and could handle the pressure of the race-track as well.

In August of 1976, Tex Cauthen took Steve to Saratoga, New York. The race meeting at Saratoga each summer is rich with tradition and prestige. Many of racing's best can be found in that small upstate New York town during the month of August. Many professional horse people go to Saratoga each year for a combination of business and holiday.

Saratoga is the site of the famous annual yearling sales, where high prices are paid for young horses in the hopes of finding a future winner. Saratoga is the place where many horsemen bring their two-year-olds to race and get experience at the track. With hope of future greatness making up a major part of the atmosphere at Saratoga, it was fitting that young

Cauthen's brief visit to that track marked a turning point in the jockey's career.

It was at Saratoga that Steve Cauthen first met Lenny Goodman. Tex Cauthen approached Goodman, one of the greatest of today's agents for race riders, to see if he would consider handling Steve. A jockey's agent is a very important person in that rider's career. It is the agent who gets the horses for the jockey to ride. A good agent can do much to promote a rider's success, and Lenny Goodman was better than good. He was the best.

Steve rode two horses that day at Saratoga. Goodman was impressed by what he saw, even though neither of the horses was a winner. Goodman told Tex Cauthen that he would be interested in working with Steve if he ever came to New York to live. The Cauthens were pleased that the agent thought Steve was worth the effort. Goodman rarely had time for a beginning jockey.

Steve's first stop after River Downs and Saratoga was not New York, however. Tex and

Myra Cauthen didn't know anyone in New York who could keep Steve and watch over him. So, they sent Steve to Chicago instead, where he could stay with a family friend who was a trainer at the Arlington Park track. Handled by agent Paul Blair, who was known for working with young riders, Steve won 40 out of the 164 races he rode at Arlington Park. Steve then returned to Churchill Downs for the fall meeting. He continued to gain more experience and his reputation grew.

In December 1976, Steve Cauthen moved his career to New York's Aqueduct Race Track and agent Lenny Goodman. It was time for him to ride with the best. Winter racing in New York is a cold, rough business. The weather is often extremely harsh, but the track is kept open. The track's business is mainly to make money, not to give pleasure. Against this dreary background, Steve Cauthen brought a new excitement to the winter racing scene. Steve was the talk of the town.

Steve on his way to Aqueduct for a day's work, bundled up against the cold.

Goodman was able to get good mounts for Cauthen at Aqueduct, and Steve won with enough of them to encourage more and more trainers to seek him out. Steve won 29 races in three weeks during that December. Racing fans began to ask for the horses ridden by the young jockey as they placed their bets. Those who bet against him and lost were described by their friends as having been "Cauthenized."

Steve Cauthen finished 1976 with more than a million dollars in purses won—$1,244,423 to be exact. He had been riding in races for just eight months. By the time he was ready to go home to Walton, Kentucky to spend Christmas with his family, Steve Cauthen was a star.

When a reporter asked the boy why he hadn't planned something more exciting than going home to his family, the young jockey is said to have replied, "What could be more exciting than that?" Steve's answer tells a lot about what matters to him.

Celebrating Christmas 1976. Father Tex is at the left, 14-year-old brother Doug is next, then Steve and his mother Myra. Eight-year-old brother Kerry is in front.

Christmas 1976 was a happy time at the Cauthen house. The entire family was enjoying Steve's success. Doug and Kerry were glad to have their brother home again. Doug, who at thirteen already knew he was going to be too large to be a jockey, was proud of his older brother's accomplishments. Kerry, age eight, delighted in teasing Steve and playing good-natured jokes on him.

Steve's incredible success at the track, his extraordinary earnings for one so young, and the great fame he had acquired almost overnight did not seem to affect his family life. The Cauthens were a close-knit group before Steve hit the big time. They still are.

After Christmas, Steve took up his winning ways at Aqueduct again. Trainers begged Goodman to put Steve on their horses. Racing fans kept talking about "the Kid" and following his every move at the track. TV and newspaper reporters covered all his activities, from his arrival at the track each morning, until the last race was over.

Steve did more than just win races at Aqueduct. He created an air of excitement about the track. He made New York racing really come alive. People who had never followed the horses before were beginning to talk about this sensational kid who had come from Kentucky to New York and turned the racing world around.

Steve was setting new track records. On January 10, 1977, Steve started a record-breaking

Getting cleaned up after a ride on a muddy track.

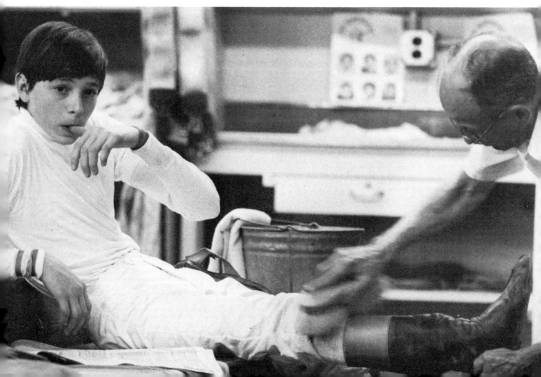

Waiting for the next race.

week. He won 23 races in one week, breaking Angel Cordero's record of 22 wins, set three years before. And in setting his record, Steve won five races in one day—two days in a row! For a jockey to win five races in a row is unusual. To do this two days in a row is almost unheard of.

A week later, on a Saturday afternoon, Cauthen had another exciting winning day. He rode in nine races, the full card at Aqueduct. He won six of the races, and finished either second or third in the other three. The six victories in one day—an accomplishment which Steve later repeated twice—tied an Aqueduct track record.

Steve's work for the weekend was still not done. Most people would have taken a rest after a day like that, but not Steve Cauthen. He got on a plane, flew to Los Angeles, California, and rode in four races on Sunday afternoon at Santa Anita Race Track. Steve won one race there, came in third in another, and turned around to catch the Sunday night plane back to New York so he could ride at Aqueduct on Monday.

Affirmed gets a pat on the neck after winning the Hollywood Derby at Hollywood Park, California, on April 16, 1977.

This was the first of many weekends when Steve raced in New York on Saturday, Los Angeles on Sunday, and back in New York on Monday. Such a work schedule would wear out many people, but for Steve Cauthen it was a chance to do what he loved best. Steve is one of those lucky people for whom work is also a great pleasure. Racing is his life, and a good life he finds it to be.

Steve's star kept rising. There seemed to be almost no limit to what the Kid could accomplish. Many people commented that only two things, serious injury, or growing too big, could stop Steve now. Would he grow too large to be a jockey? That didn't appear to be a possibility in the near future. His five-foot-one-inch tall frame with 94 pounds or so didn't seem in danger of growing too big, although his large, strong hands and feet were a hint that it could happen some day.   C869068   CO. SCHOOLS

More likely than growing too big was the possibility of an injury. That's a risk all jockeys have to live with. Racing is a dangerous sport, both for the riders and for their horses. Somewhere in the back of every jockey's mind must be the notion that serious injury could occur.

And a bad spill was one experience that Steve hadn't had—yet.

Steve didn't seem to be at all worried about the risks he was taking as a jockey. He spoke lightly about the possibility of a bad fall, and said that he had been landing on his head ever since he was a little kid. Steve's mother probably did worry more than anyone else in the family, but

Getting ready to go out there and win . . . and he did.

she knew that worry wouldn't change things. Tex Cauthen had been around race tracks long enough to know what the risks were, but he had confidence in his son. He knew that Steve would cope with whatever came his way.

It was on May 23, 1977 that the racing world got its chance to find out how Steve Cauthen would react to a bad spill and injury. In the fourth race at Belmont Park in New York, Steve was aboard Bay Streak, a horse who usually ran strongly at the finish. Bay Streak was moving up after the last turn, headed toward the finish line in what looked like a winning stretch drive. And then it happened. Bay Streak snapped a leg, stumbled, and went down. The horse behind him, ridden by Jorge Valasquez, also went down. A third horse and rider added to the crash.

Both Valasquez and Cauthen were hurt and were taken to the hospital. Steve suffered a broken arm right above the wrist, two broken fingers and a broken rib. He needed ten stitches in his head and fifteen in his arm. And he had a severe concussion and was unconscious for the trip to the hospital. When he woke up, he was still trying to figure out what had happened. But he didn't feel scared. He did admit to confusion, but not to fear.

Steve and his parents knew that he would ride again as soon as he could. Other people wondered, but the Cauthens knew that Steve would be back.

It was exactly a month later, on June 23rd, that everyone else knew also. The place was again New York's Belmont Park. The name of the horse was Little Miracle, and many people felt that it was an appropriate name. In his first race after recovery from his injuries, Steve rode perfectly, and guided Little Miracle—a half-brother to Affirmed—to victory while the crowd cheered. Steve Cauthen had come back.

Steve's successes continued. At Saratoga in August 1977, he set another record—300 wins in a New York season.

As Steve's success and fame increased,

Steve rides to his 300th win in 1977, aboard Gun Blast at Belmont on July 7th.

agent Lenny Goodman was working on getting the highest quality horses for his young charge to ride. While Steve rode in many an ordinary race, he also won 23 stakes races in 1977. This included the $200,000 Washington, D.C. International, a very important race which Steve won on a horse named Johnny D, against very strong opposition. Steve remembers this race as one of the highlights of his racing career. Johnny D had not been expected to win, and Cauthen's clever, competent riding seemed to give the edge the horse needed.

It was in 1977 that Cauthen began to ride Affirmed, then a two-year-old. Their first race together was in the Sanford Stakes at Saratoga, and they won. This was the beginning of the story of the team of Cauthen and Affirmed, a combination that was to go far.

The rivalry between the two outstanding horses, Affirmed and Alydar, began when they were both racing as two-year-olds. Cauthen rode Affirmed to victory over Alydar in the Sanford

Stakes and Belmont Futurity. Alydar beat Affirmed in the Champagne Stakes, a race of great prestige. When the Champagne Stakes was over, Alydar had won two of the contests between them and Affirmed had won three. The last contest between the two horses that year was the Laurel Futurity, which was billed as the match to settle the championship for two-year-olds. It was a close race, with Cauthen riding Affirmed to a win over Alydar by a neck.

After their exciting season as two-year-olds, both Affirmed and Alydar were recognized as extremely fine horses. The score for their rivalry in six contests stood 4 to 2, with Affirmed ahead of Alydar. The stage was set for a winter of wondering which colt would be the better three-year-old.

During the winter of 1977, Steve Cauthen rode regularly and won many races—a total of 487 for the year. He was called the "Six-Million-Dollar-Man," because his mounts had won more than that amount in purses during 1977. Steve's share of these purses was ten percent, or more than $600,000. Even after agent Lenny Goodman received his fee, which amounted to a fourth of the jockey's earnings, there was plenty of money. Steve didn't waste his winnings, and most of the money went right into the bank. The Cauthens had all been in the uncertain world of racing long enough to know that saving for the future was the wisest thing to do. Hopefully Steve would race and be successful for a long time, but one could never be sure.

As 1977 drew to a close, Steve was being hailed from coast to coast as an outstanding athlete. In a year, he had changed from an apprentice jockey to an internationally known and respected sportsman. He was interviewed and written up again and again. People just didn't seem to get tired of reading and hearing about "the Kid." Through it all, Steve remained himself —a nice person who did his job well.

In December of 1977, Steve Cauthen won the Seagram's Seven Crowns of Sports Jockey of the Year award. The Seven Crowns of Sports

Surrounded by members of the press for an interview. The Kid is big news.

competition uses a computer to analyze performance of athletes in seven different sports. Jockey performance ratings are based on the results of races. Races of high quality—those with bigger purses, more difficult competition, and longer distances—are worth more points in the analysis than easier races.

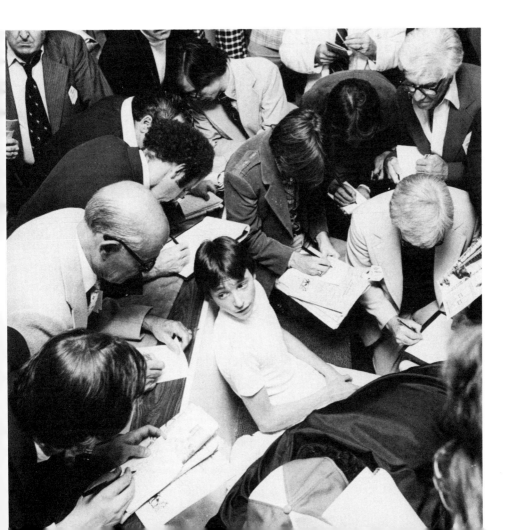

At New York City's famous 21-Club, when retired jockey great Eddie Arcaro presented the Seven Crowns of Sports trophy and a check for $10,000 to Cauthen, the young jockey demonstrated his poise and maturity as he was pressed for comments by representatives of the various news media. Many reporters asked Steve what it felt like to have so much money and fame. He answered the questions politely, but seemed unimpressed by all this attention. Steve handles interviews and meetings with the media as smoothly as he handles a spirited race horse. But one gets the feeling that if he were forced to choose between fame and riding a horse, Steve would prefer to ride a horse. Riding is far more than a job for Steve Cauthen. He loves horses and has an extraordinary communication with the animals.

The day following the presentation of the Seven Crowns award, Steve Cauthen was pictured on the cover of Sports Illustrated magazine, which presented the young jockey with its Sportsman of the Year Award. This honor is given to the outstanding athlete of the year, with all

Eddie Arcaro, himself a great jockey, presents the Seagram's Seven Crowns of Sports trophy to The Kid.

sports being considered in the competition. The magazine story about Cauthen said that, ". . . at the age of 17 he has accomplished more in a year than any jockey in history." The article went on to mention ". . . that already there exists the mad school of thought that this little boy is the finest rider of all time."

If you passed Steve Cauthen on the street and gave a quick glance, you might then think he was still a child. He looks so young. To talk to him and to see him ride, however, would convince any person quickly that here is an outstanding young man. One racing fan described Cauthen as "the biggest little man in the world." The description seems to fit.

During the early months of 1978, as Steve went on riding and winning, talk in sports circles turned to the upcoming Kentucky Derby, an event that means a lot to the racing world. Steve Cauthen would ride Affirmed.

By the time Derby Day rolled around both Steve Cauthen and Affirmed were ready. At post time, 5:41 on May 6, all the planning and predicting and talk were put aside. It was time for one

Fellow jockeys sing "Happy Birthday" to Steve as he turned 18. The scene is the jockey room at Aqueduct, the jockeys are, left to right, Nick Santagata, Jorge Velasquez, Robert McNight, Steve, Jean Cruguet, and Angel Santiago.

moment of truth—the big race itself. In the field of eleven hopefuls, Cauthen guided Affirmed to a length-and-a-half victory over second-place Alydar. It was a great day for Affirmed and Cauthen, for trainer Lazaro "Laz" Barrera and for the horse's owners, Patrice and Louis Wolfson. The victory was especially sweet for Patrice Wolfson, whose father Hirsch Jacobs had been

Trainer Laz Berrera, owner Louis Wolfson, and jockey Steve Cauthen.

an extremely successful and famous trainer, but a trainer who had never had a Derby winner during his long career.

As soon as the Derby was over, attention turned to the Preakness, second race in the Triple

ouis and Patrice Wolfson, owners
f Affirmed, greet Steve after the
¨entucky Derby win.

Crown. Would Affirmed be able to do it again? Or, would Alydar prove to be the stronger of the two this time? The Preakness, run three weeks after the Kentucky Derby at Pimlico Race Track in Maryland, is a sixteenth of a mile longer than the Derby. Would Alydar, a strong stretch runner, cope with the longer distance better than Affirmed? The racing world again waited eagerly for some answers.

The Preakness, like the Kentucky Derby before it, turned into an exciting stretch duel between Affirmed and Alydar. At the wire, it was once again Affirmed, this time by a neck. Many thought Alydar could have caught Affirmed had the race been just a few strides longer. But Steve Cauthen knew that what mattered was the finish line, and at *that* point his horse had been ahead. Cauthen and Affirmed had won the race, and all the morning-after comments in the world couldn't take that away from them. But the third leg of the Triple Crown, the Belmont Stakes, was a longer race—a mile and a half. The Preakness

A big smile of victory as a groom leads Affirmed to the Winner's Circle after the Preakness, May 20, 1978.

had been even closer—a neck. Would Affirmed be able to hold on and win the Belmont Stakes? Steve Cauthen thought so. Some others were not sure. Would Alydar find that the longer distance in the Belmont would give him the room he needed to catch Affirmed?

At Belmont Park, Affirmed went to the post as a popular favorite, even though some experts doubted his ability to beat Alydar at that distance. Saturday, June 10th was the big day. The starting gate opened, and the horses were off. Steve got Affirmed into an early lead. Could he hold it? Alydar came up quickly and once again the race was between the two horses, Affirmed and Alydar.

With a furlong to go in the Belmont, Alydar's nose was slightly ahead of Affirmed. But Steve used his whip carefully and at just the right time. Those many long hours on the bales of hay in the barn so many years ago now paid off. Steve was able to get just a little more from his horse, and at the wire it was Affirmed by a head. The final half mile had been run in a record 49.4 seconds. No horse had finished faster in the 109 years that there had been a Belmont Stakes. The Kid and the amazing horse had done it again.

Steve Cauthen had done what few others had done in racing history. He had won the Triple Crown. And he had done it when he was only 18

Steve rides Affirmed to a close victory over Alydar in the Belmont Stakes, June 10, 1978.

years old, in his first attempt. From apprentice jockey to Sportsman of the Year and winner of the Triple Crown! Steve Cauthen seemed almost superhuman.

After the Belmont Stakes, Steve Cauthen continued to ride at Belmont and to bring home his share of winners. Then on the sixth of July, Lenny Goodman, Steve's agent, suffered a heart attack. Steve missed an important source of support and encouragement in his life. The Kid, upset about Goodman's illness, went into a bit of a slump. He wasn't winning quite so often as he was used to. In August, Cauthen went to Saratoga to ride in the summer meeting there. Goodman, who was still recovering from his illness, was permitted to spend one hour a day at the track working with his star jockey. The future looked brighter.

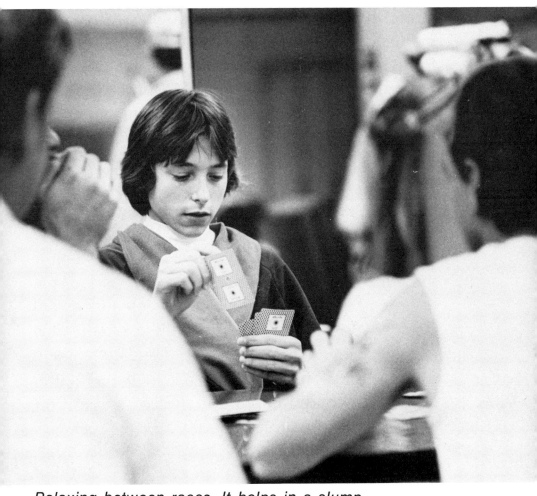

Relaxing between races. It helps in a slump.

On August 9, 1978, Cauthen was scheduled to ride in seven of the nine races on the Saratoga card. In the third race, Steve was aboard a horse called Cute As A Button. At about the quarter pole (a quarter of a mile from the finish line), Cute As A Button stumbled and went down. Cauthen was tossed over the horse's head and rolled under the rail to safety, but he had been hurt. A separated shoulder would keep him out of action until September.

Some people feared that this accident—the second of Steve's career—would cause him to come back a more timid and less successful rider. In September, Steve Cauthen once again rode at Belmont. He won. The Kid had come back again. And he had come back in time for the Marlboro Cup, an important stakes race at Belmont, with a purse of $300,000.

Affirmed, the Triple Crown winner for 1978, was going against Alydar and Seattle Slew, the Triple Crown winner just a year earlier. In the more than 100 years that racing has had the

At Saratoga on August 9, 1978, Cauthen hits the track after his mount, Cute as a Button, stumbles and falls.

Steve begins to roll clear of the oncoming horses.

three events for the Triple Crown, only a dozen horses have managed to win all three of them. And the happening of two Triple Crown winners back to back—Seattle Slew in 1977 and Affirmed

in 1978—was most unusual. Which of the three
was the best horse?

He rolls under the rail to safety in the track's infield.

But things did not turn out as planned. Alydar fractured his foot and couldn't run. So the race became a contest between the four-year-old Seattle Slew and the three-year-old Affirmed. The crowd sent Affirmed to the post as the favorite. Both sentiment and betting dollars were clearly on the side of Steve Cauthen and Affirmed. Seattle Slew hadn't accomplished much since his Triple Crown victory more than a year earlier. The horse had been sick and had disappointed many of his fans. Affirmed, on the other hand, appeared to be in the best condition of his racing career.

The starting gate opened and the horses were off. Right from the start it was Seattle Slew. He took the lead immediately and he kept it. The crowd wasn't worried. At any moment jockey Cauthen would make his move on Affirmed and catch the leader. Or would he? Cauthen did make his move, but Seattle Slew was equal to it. The older horse held the lead and widened it. At the wire it was Seattle Slew by three lengths.

Steve Cauthen was still "the Kid." But this race clearly showed something very important about the young jockey. It showed him to be human. In racing there may be good bets, but there are no sure things—not even with a great like Steve Cauthen.

"The Kid."

PHOTO CREDITS

UPI Photos: pp. 6, 9, 12, 17, 20, 22, 30, 31, 34, 36, 39, 43, 47, 48, 49, 51, 53, 55
Liz Naples: pp. 57, 58, 59

Glossary of Racing Terms

Apprentice—a beginning jockey. A jockey with more than a year's experience or 40 wins is no longer considered an apprentice.

Furlong—one-eighth of a mile. The distance of a horse race is expressed in furlongs.

In the Money—1st, 2nd, and 3rd horses in a race.

Length—the length of a horse. A horse that wins by two lengths is ahead of the horse that comes in second by a distance that equals the length of two horses.

Out of the Money—a losing horse, 4th place or worse.

Paddock—the enclosed area in which horses are saddled and mounted before a race.

Place—the horse that comes in second in a race. Wins less prize money for owners and bettors than the first place horse.

Run for the Roses—the Kentucky Derby, so named because a blanket of roses is placed around the neck of the winning horse.

Show—third place, but still in the money for owners and bettors.

Stretch—the last part of a race. A good stretch runner is a horse that comes on strong at the finish.

Triple Crown—three important races for three-year-olds: the Kentucky Derby, the Preakness, and the Belmont Stakes.

Wire—the finish line of a race.

Yearling—a one-year-old horse.